of co-ordination

imp
devel
for ins
the first book of the eight book series.

This series provides an enjoyable intro-
duction to poetry, music and dance for
every young child. Most books of this
type have only a few rhymes for each
age group, whereas each book of this
series is intended for a particular age
group. There is a strong teaching sequence
in the selection of rhymes, from the
first simple ways of winning the child's
interest by toe tapping and palm
tickling jingles, through practice in
numbers, memory and pronunciation,
to combining sound, action and
words. For the first time young
children can learn rhymes
in a sequence that is
related to their age.

•❧O❧•

Contents

Page

4   Round and round the garden

8   Ring the bell

10   Here is the church and here is the steeple

12   Robert Barnes, fellow fine

14   This little pig went to market

18   Put your finger in Foxy's hole

20   There were two blackbirds

24   This pig went to the barn

26   Pat-a-cake, pat-a-cake

30   Pease porridge hot

32   Incy wincy spider

36   Here are the lady's knives and forks

38   I'm a little teapot, short and stout

40   Five currant buns in a baker's shop

44   My mother said that if I should

48   Here sits the Lord Mayor

50   Dance Thumbkin dance

LEARNING WITH TRADITIONAL RHYMES

Finger Rhymes

by DOROTHY and JOHN TAYLOR
with illustrations by BRIAN PRICE THOMAS
and photographs by JOHN MOYES

Ladybird Books Loughborough

Round and round the garden

Round and round the garden

Like a teddy bear;
  Run forefinger round the palm.

One step, two step,
  Jump finger up the arm.

Tickle you under there.
  Tickle under the arm.

Round and round the garden
Like a teddy bear;
One step, two step,
Tickle you under there.

6

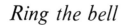

Ring the bell

Ring the bell,
    Tug a lock of hair.

Knock at the door,
    Tap forehead.

Peep in,
    Peer into eyes.

Lift the latch,
    Tweak nose.

Walk in.
    Open mouth.

Here is the church and here is the steeple

Here is the church, and here is the steeple;

Open the door and here are the people.

Here is the parson going upstairs,

And here he is a-saying his prayers.

Child's actions

Line 1 (a) *Interlock fingers, with palms uppermost, then turn over so that knuckles form the ridge of the church roof.*

(b) *Raise little fingers, tips touching.*

Line 2 (a) *Part thumbs to open the door.*

(b) *Turn hands inside out to show the congregation (fingers).*

Line 3 *Make a ladder of the left hand fingers and walk the right thumb and forefinger up.*

Line 4 *Put hands together as for prayer.*

11

Robert Barnes, fellow fine

Robert Barnes, fellow fine,
Pat sole of left foot, following the rhythm of the words.

Can you shoe this horse of mine?
Pat sole of right foot.

Yes, good sir, that I can,
Pat sole of left foot.

As well as any other man.
Pat sole of right foot.

There's a nail and there's a prod,
Pretend to take a nail and hammer it in.

And now, good sir, your horse is shod.
Bang both feet together.

This little pig went to market

This little pig went to market,
Grasp big toe.

This little pig stayed at home,
Grasp second toe.

This little pig had roast beef,
Grasp third toe.

This little pig had none,
Grasp fourth toe.

And this little pig cried: Wee-wee-wee,
Grasp little toe.

I can't find my way home.
Tickle underneath the foot.

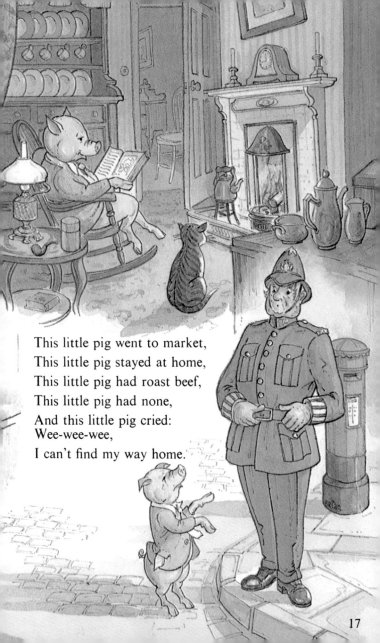

This little pig went to market,
This little pig stayed at home,
This little pig had roast beef,
This little pig had none,
And this little pig cried:
Wee-wee-wee,
I can't find my way home.

Put your finger in Foxy's hole

Put your finger in Foxy's hole,

Foxy's not at home;

Foxy's at the back door,

Picking a marrow bone.

Mother's actions

With palms facing, interlock the tips of the fingers leaving a gap in the middle to represent Foxy's hole.
Line 1 Child puts a finger into the hole.
*   4 Bring thumbs together to lightly pinch child's finger.*
Then change roles and let the child play Foxy.

There were two blackbirds

There were two blackbirds
Hold up both forefingers.

Sitting on a hill,

The one named Jack,
Wag right finger.

The other named Jill.
Wag left finger.

Fly away, Jack!
Hide right finger behind back or behind table.

Fly away, Jill!
Hide left finger behind back or behind table.

Come again, Jack!
Bring back right finger.

Come again, Jill!
Bring back left finger.

There were two blackbirds   Fly away, Jack!
Sitting on a hill,   Fly away, Jill!
The one named Jack,   Come again, Jack!
The other named Jill.   Come again, Jill!

This pig went to the barn

This pig went to the barn,
Grasp big toe.

This ate all the corn,
Grasp second toe.

This said he would tell,
Grasp third toe.

This said he wasn't well,
Grasp fourth toe.

This went week! week! week! over the door sill.
Grasp little toe, then tickle underneath the foot.

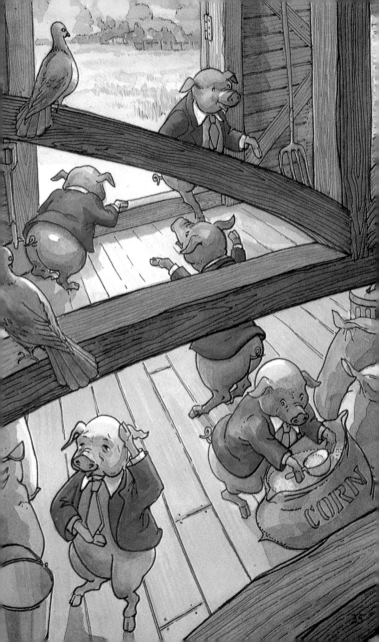

Pat-a-cake, pat-a-cake

Pat-a-cake, pat-a-cake,

Baker's man,

Bake me a cake

As fast as you can.

Pat it and prick it

And mark it with 'B',

And put it in the oven

For Baby and me.

Mother's actions

Clasp hands together following the exact rhythm of the words, e.g. pat-a-cake, pat-a-cake . . .

Pat-a-cake, pat-a-cake,
Baker's man,
Bake me a cake
As fast as you can.
Pat it and prick it
And mark it with 'B'
And put it in the oven
For Baby and me.

Pease porridge hot

Pease porridge hot,

Pease porridge cold,

Pease porridge in the pot,

Nine days old.

Some like it hot,

Some like it cold,

Some like it in the pot,

Nine days old.

Mother's or child's actions
    Clap hands together to fit the exact rhythm of words.

Alternative actions

Child with partner

With an older child, clapping hands can be more exciting if, facing a partner, both right hands are clapped together on the word hot, *left hands on* cold, *both on* old, *and so on....*

The Family

Play the game of making a pile of hands then continually draw bottom hand to top of the pile, again to the rhythm of the rhyme.

Incy wincy spider

Incy Wincy Spider,
Wriggle fingers.

Climbing up the spout,
Gradually raise arms, whilst wriggling the fingers.

Down came the rain,
Lower arms, dabbing with fingers to represent spots of rain

And washed the spider out.

Out came the sunshine,
Raise arms and spread out hands to represent sunshine.

Dried up all the rain,
Wriggle fingers.

Incy Wincy Spider,
Wriggle fingers.

Climbed the spout again.
Gradually raise arms, whilst wriggling the fingers.

Incy Wincy Spider,
Climbing up the spout,
Down came the rain,
And washed the spider out

Out came the sunshine,
Dried up all the rain,
Incy Wincy Spider,
Climbed the spout again.

Here are the lady's knives and forks

Here are the lady's knives and forks,

Interlace fingers with palms uppermost, fingertips representing knives and forks.

Here is the lady's table.

Turn hands over without unlocking fingers.

Here is the lady's looking-glass,

Raise little fingers, tips touching.

And here is the baby's cradle.

Raise forefingers and rock.

I'm a little teapot, short and stout

I'm a little teapot, short and stout;
Assume semi-crouching position.

Here's my handle,
Put one hand on hip.

Here's my spout.
Hold out other arm, bending at elbow and curving hand.

When it's teatime hear me shout,
Hold position.

'Pick me up
Hold position.

and pour me out.'
Bend body slowly to the outstretched arm side.

Five currant buns in a baker's shop

Five currant buns in a baker's shop,
Hold up five fingers.

Round and fat with sugar on the top.
Rub top of one's head.

Along came a boy with a penny one day,
Pretend to hold penny with free hand.

Bought a currant bun and took it away.
Bend little finger out of sight.

Four currant buns in a baker's shop,
Hold up four fingers and repeat actions until fourth line, when the ring finger should be bent out of sight.

Round and fat with sugar on the top.

Along came a boy with a penny one day,

Bought a currant bun and took it away.

Three currant buns, etc.
Other verses: continue subtracting fingers as before.

Five currant buns in a baker's shop,
Round and fat with sugar on the top.
Along came a boy with a penny one day,
Bought a currant bun and took it away.

43

My mother said that if I should

My mother said that if I should

Play with the gipsies in the wood,

She would say, 'You naughty girl!

You naughty girl to disobey!'

Actions
*The partners alternately clap their
own hands and each other's hands,
gradually increasing the speed as the
rhythm proceeds.*

My mother said that if I should
Play with the gipsies in the wood,
She would say, 'You naughty girl!
You naughty girl to disobey!'

46

Here sits the Lord Mayor

Here sits the Lord Mayor,
Gently tap on child's forehead.

Here sit his men,
Point to eyes.

Here sits the cockadoodle,
Touch right cheek.

Here sits the hen,
Touch left cheek.

Here sit the little chickens,
Point to teeth.

Here they run in,
Point to mouth.

Chin chopper, chin chopper,
Chuck under chin.

Chin chopper, chin.
Chuck under chin.

Dance Thumbkin dance

Dance Thumbkin dance,
Wag thumbs of both hands.

Dance Thumbkin dance,

Dance ye merry men, every one:
Wag all the fingers.

But Thumbkin he can dance alone,
Wag thumbs only.

Thumbkin, he can dance alone.

Dance *Foreman* dance,
Verse 2 Wag forefingers.

Dance *Longman* dance,
3 Wag middle fingers.

Dance *Ringman* dance,
4 Wag ring fingers.

Dance *Littleman* dance,
5 Wag little fingers.

·❧O❧·

BOOK ONE
🦋 *Finger Rhymes* 🦋

A selection of finger counting
and other rhymes to exercise the
young child's mind and body.

BOOK TWO
🦋 *Number Rhymes* 🦋

This book brings together many familiar
and some less well known rhymes which
help with the first steps of arithmetic.

BOOK THREE
🦋 *Memory Rhymes* 🦋

A diverse collection of rhymes mainly
concerned with days of the week, months
of the year, points of the compass and
letters of the alphabet.

BOOK FOUR
🦋 *Talking Rhymes* 🦋

Humorous and other verses provi-
ding practice in pronunciation,
including many of the
better known tongue-
twisters.